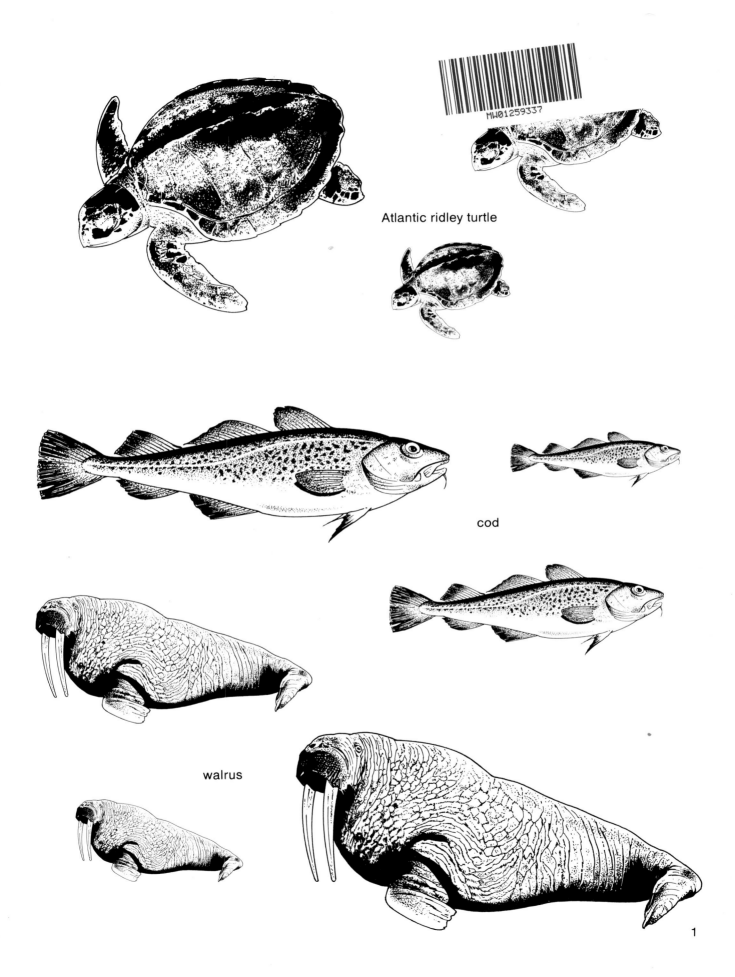

Atlantic ridley turtle

cod

walrus

great frigate bird

scallop

spotted dolphin

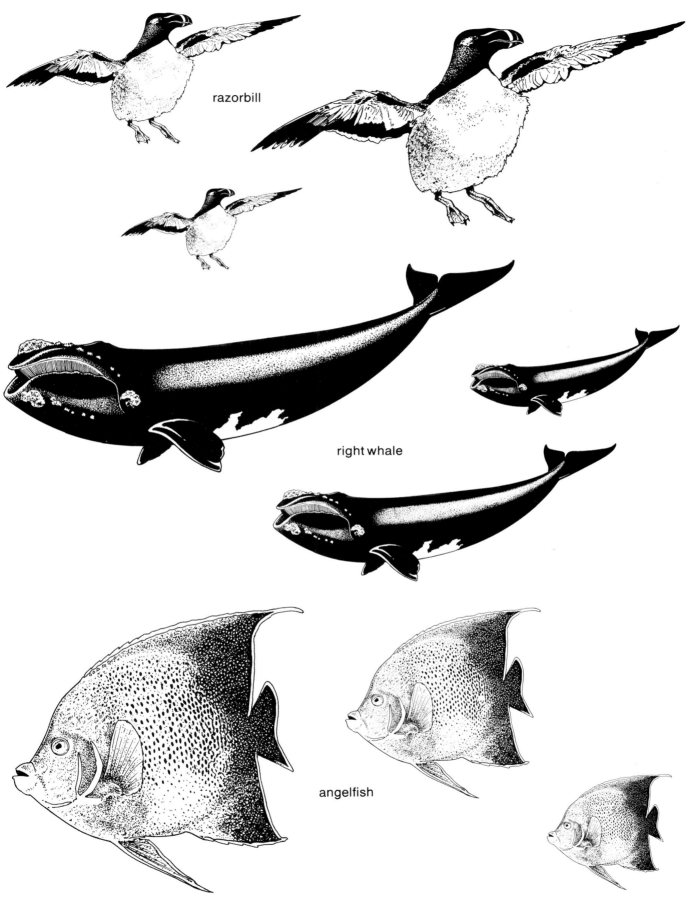

razorbill

right whale

angelfish

3

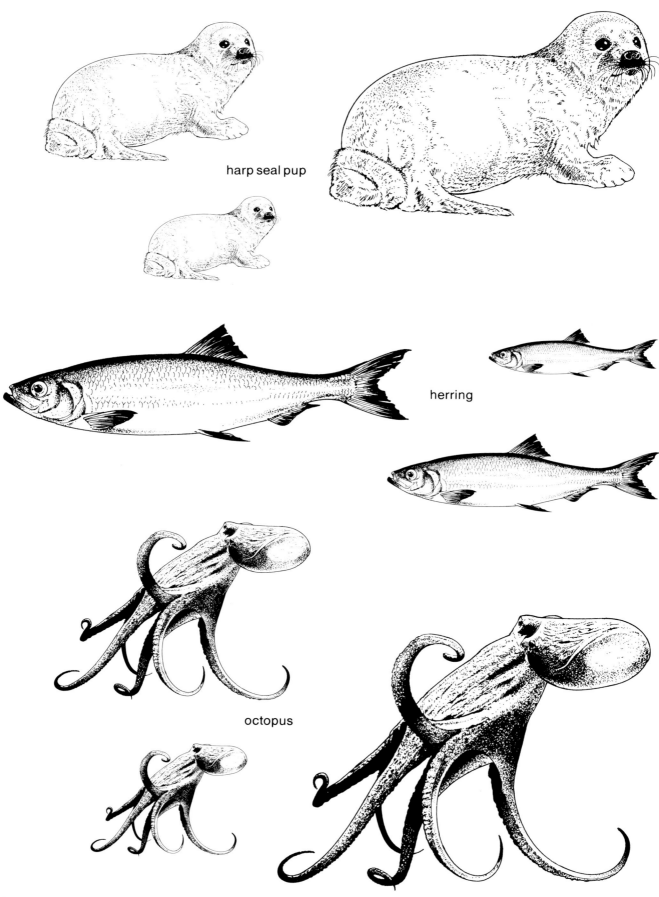

harp seal pup

herring

octopus

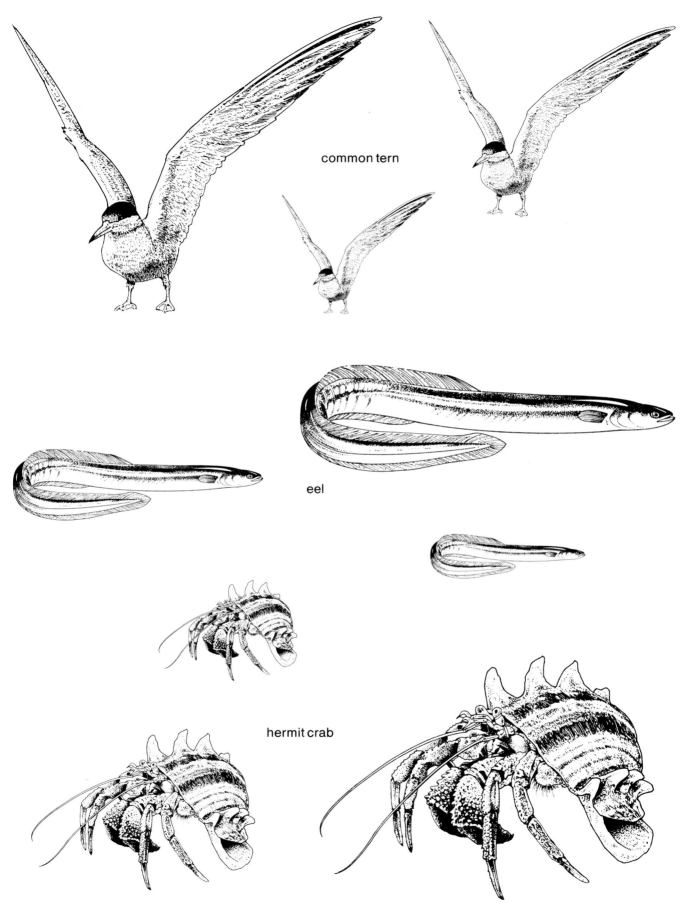

common tern

eel

hermit crab

5

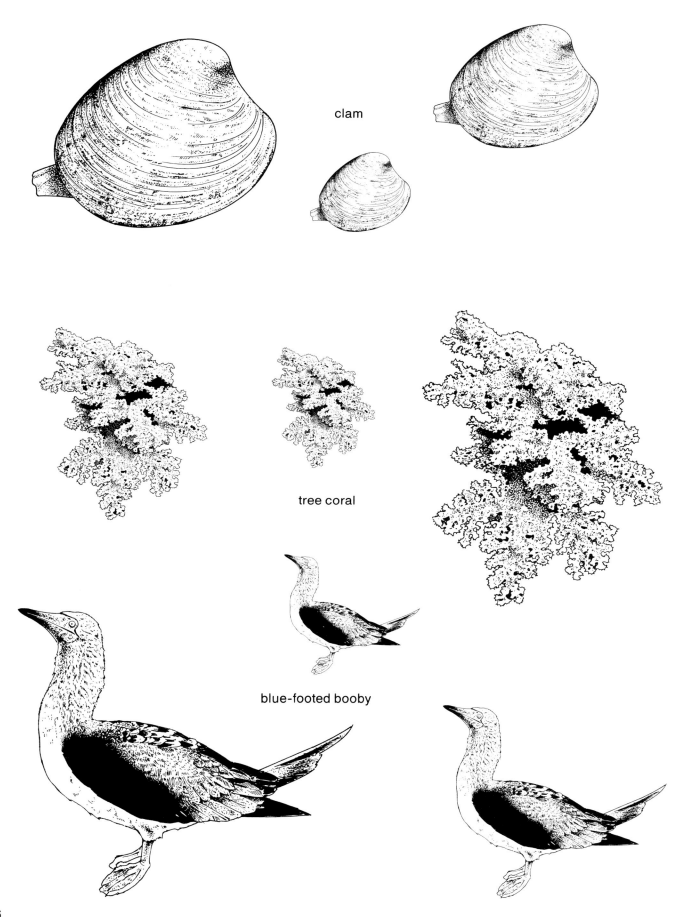

clam

tree coral

blue-footed booby

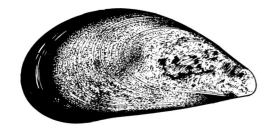

mussel

sea anemone

anchovy

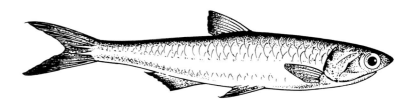

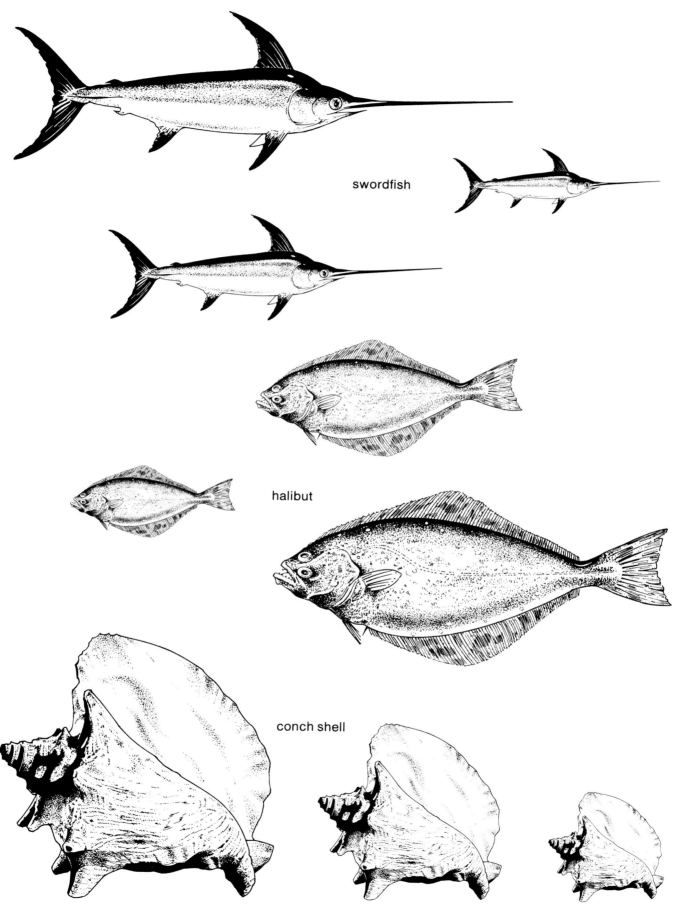

swordfish

halibut

conch shell

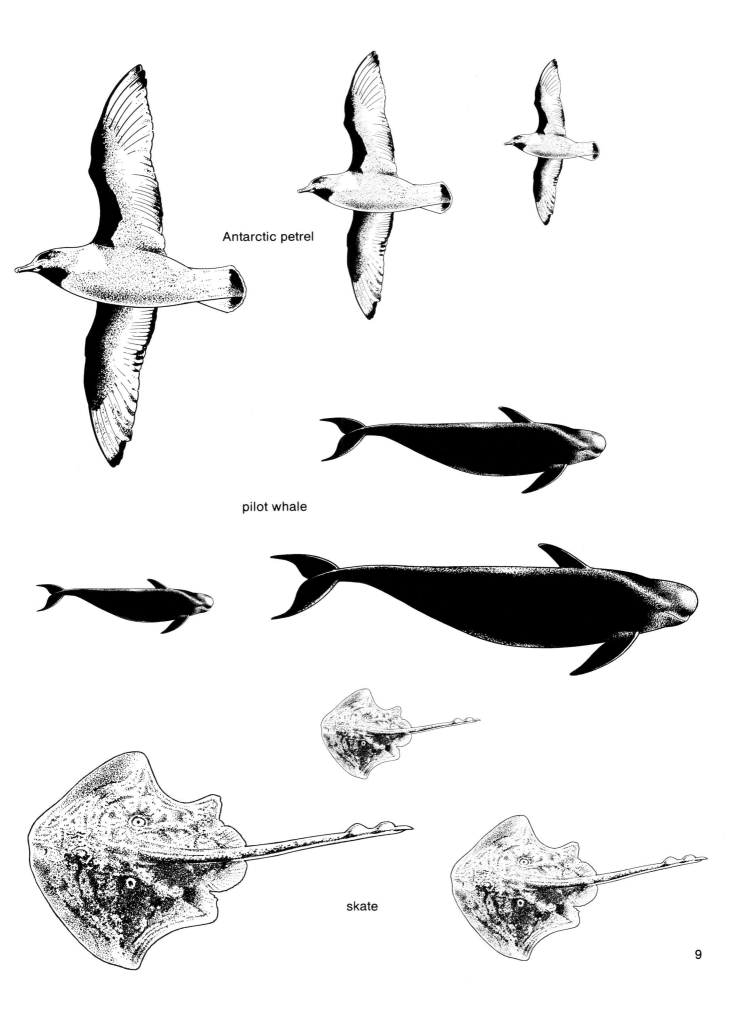

Antarctic petrel

pilot whale

skate

9

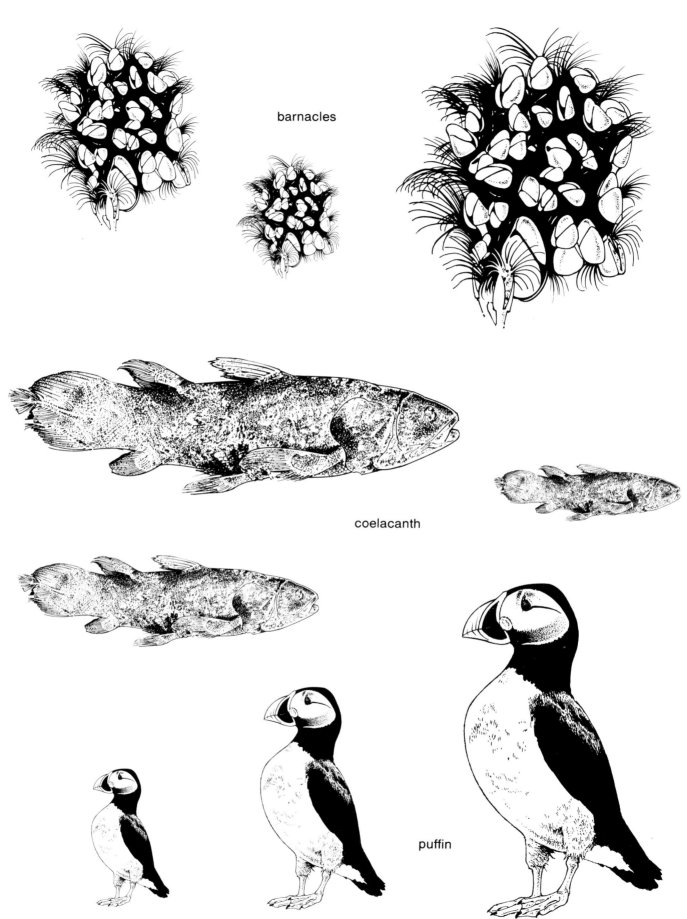

barnacles

coelacanth

puffin

oyster

hooded seal

lobster

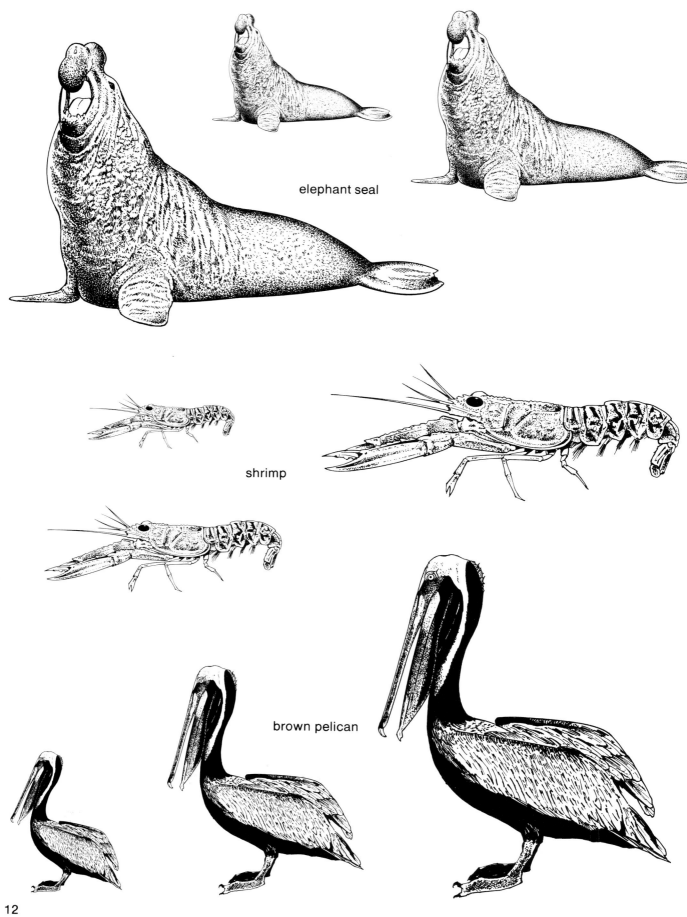

elephant seal

shrimp

brown pelican

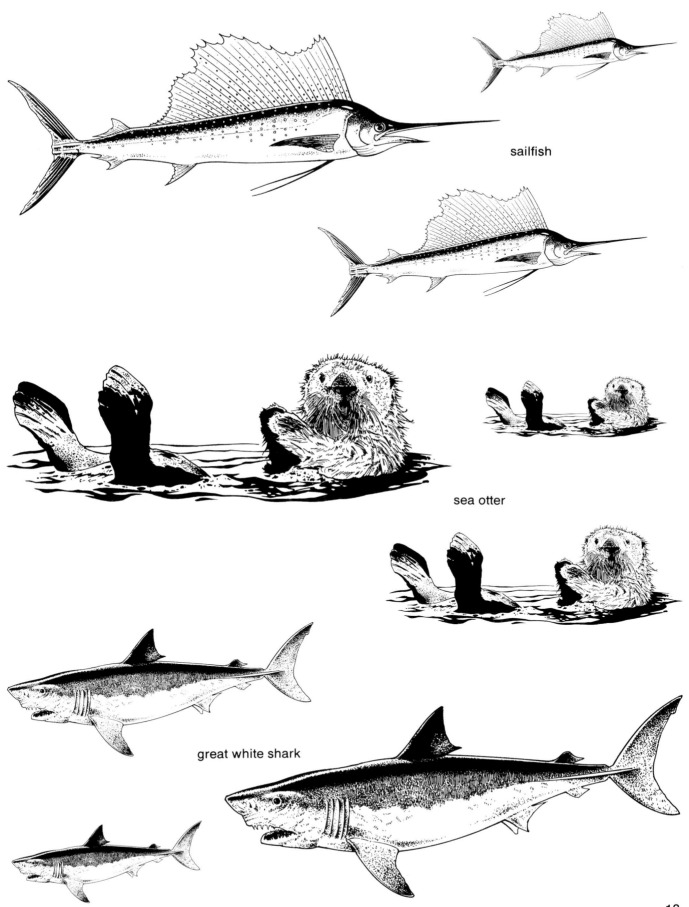

sailfish

sea otter

great white shark

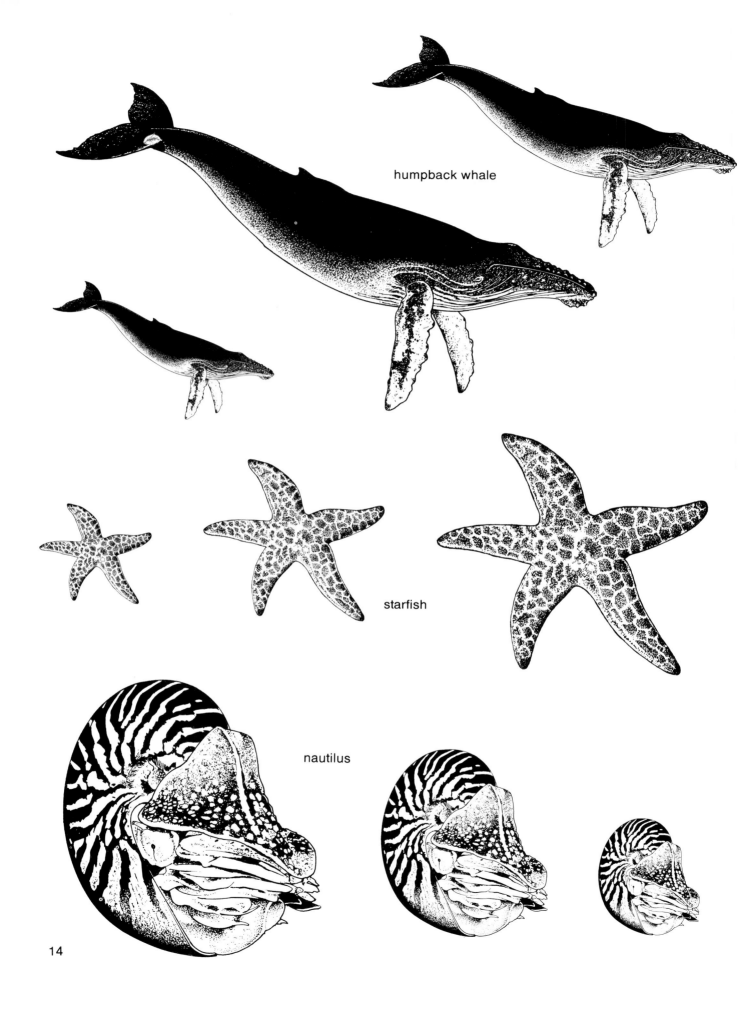

humpback whale

starfish

nautilus

14

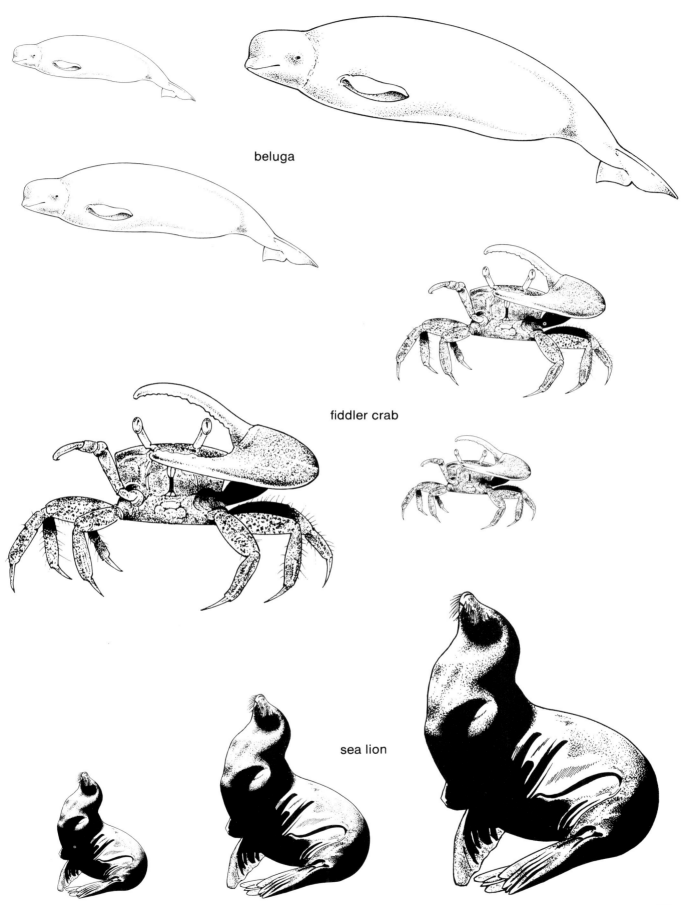

beluga

fiddler crab

sea lion

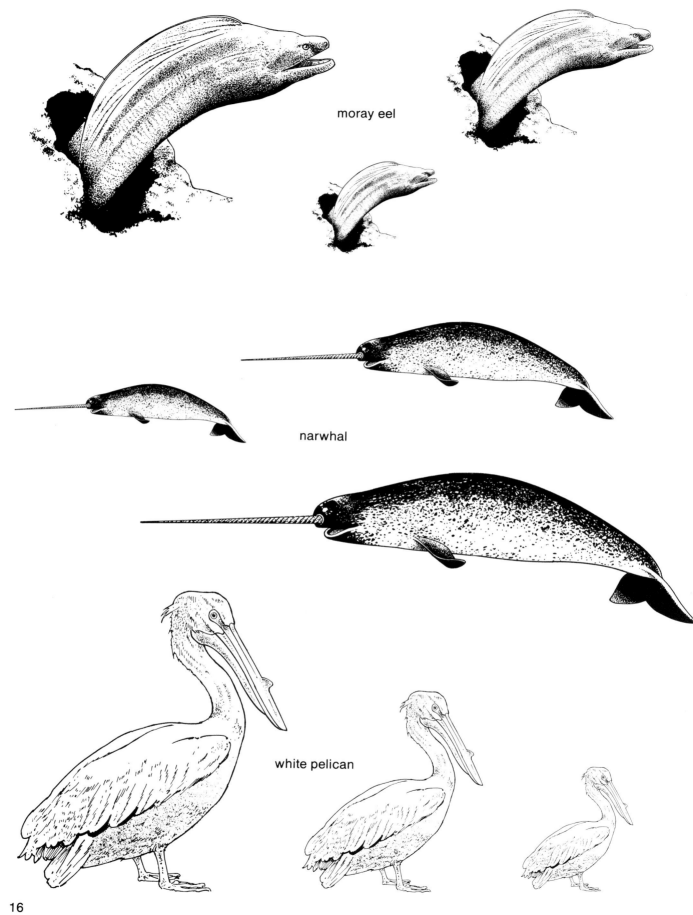

moray eel

narwhal

white pelican

16

leopard seal

emperor penguin and chick

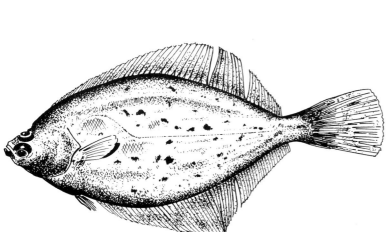
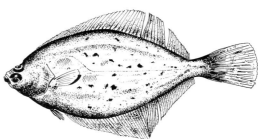

flounder

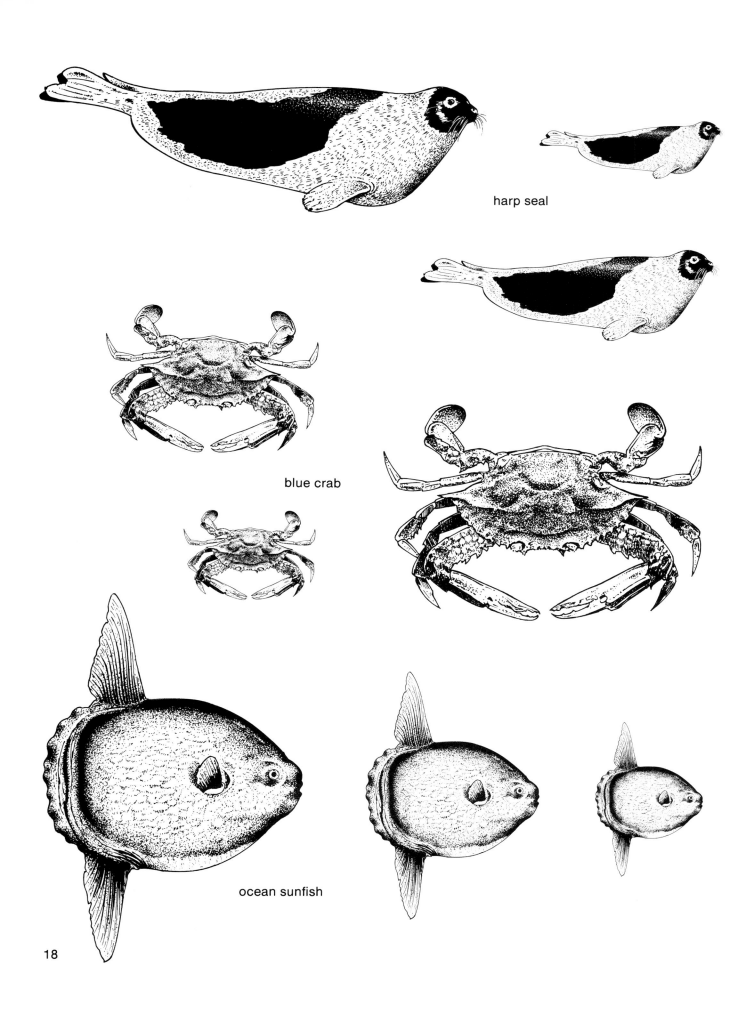

harp seal

blue crab

ocean sunfish

18

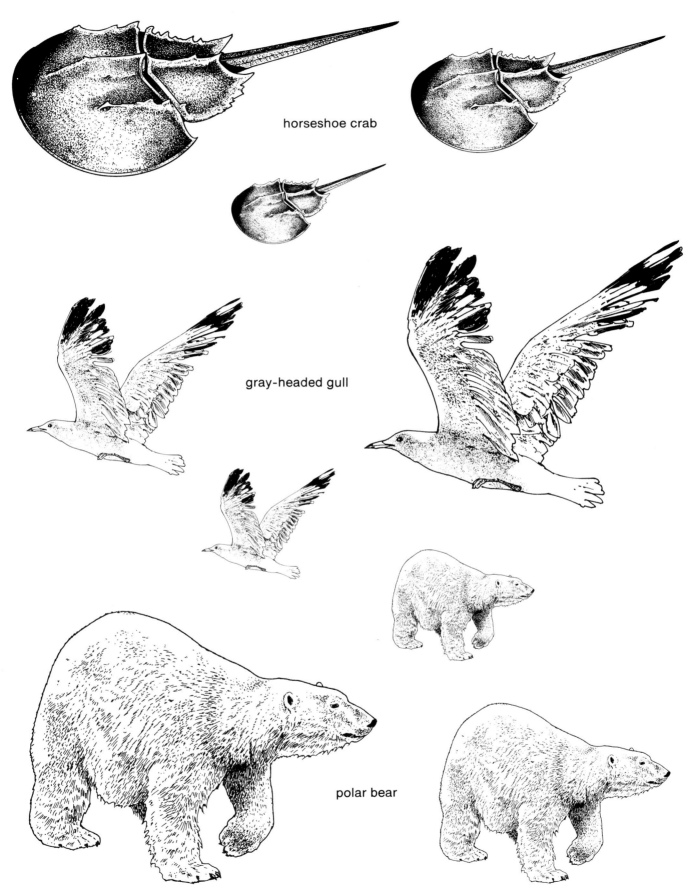

horseshoe crab

gray-headed gull

polar bear

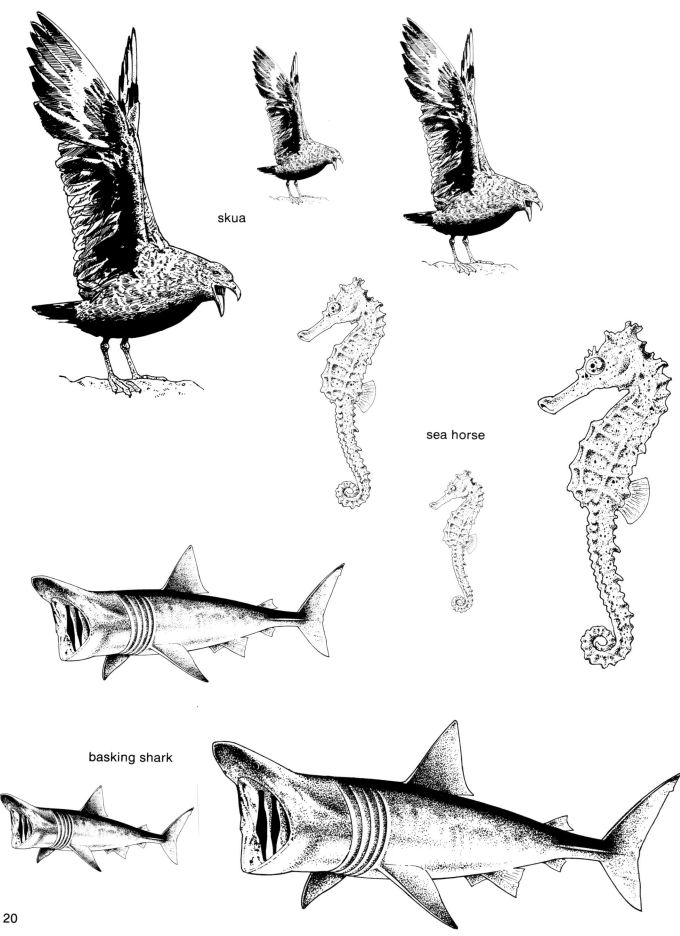

skua

sea horse

basking shark

whale shark

cuttlefish

Adélie penguin

21

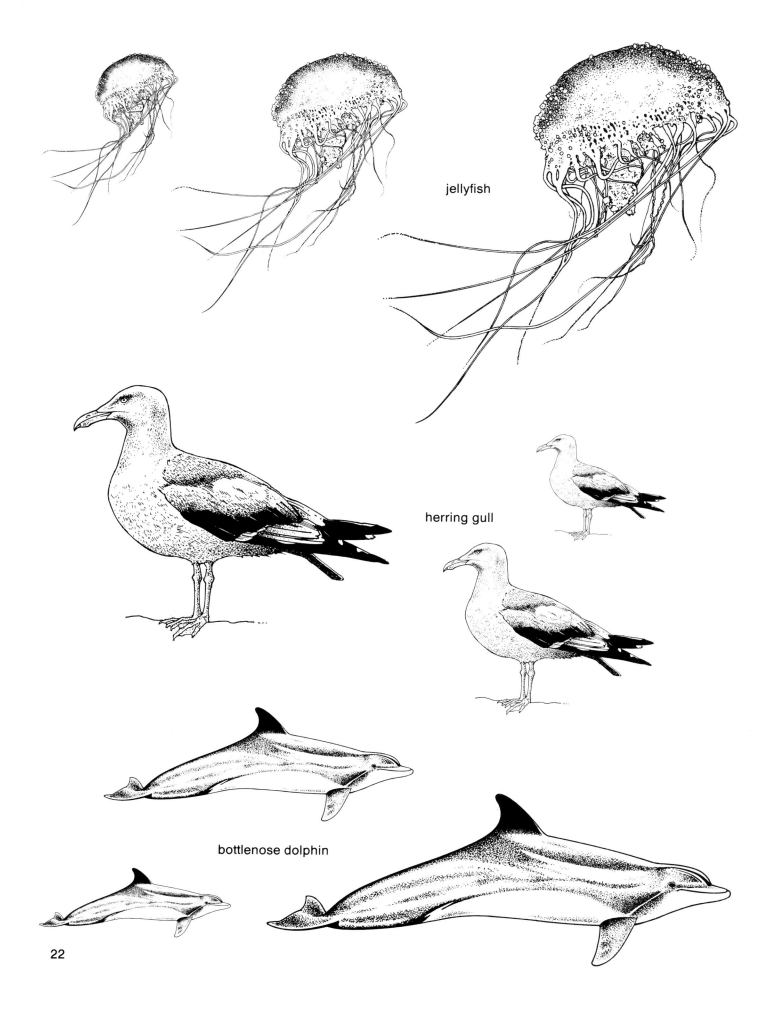

jellyfish

herring gull

bottlenose dolphin

22

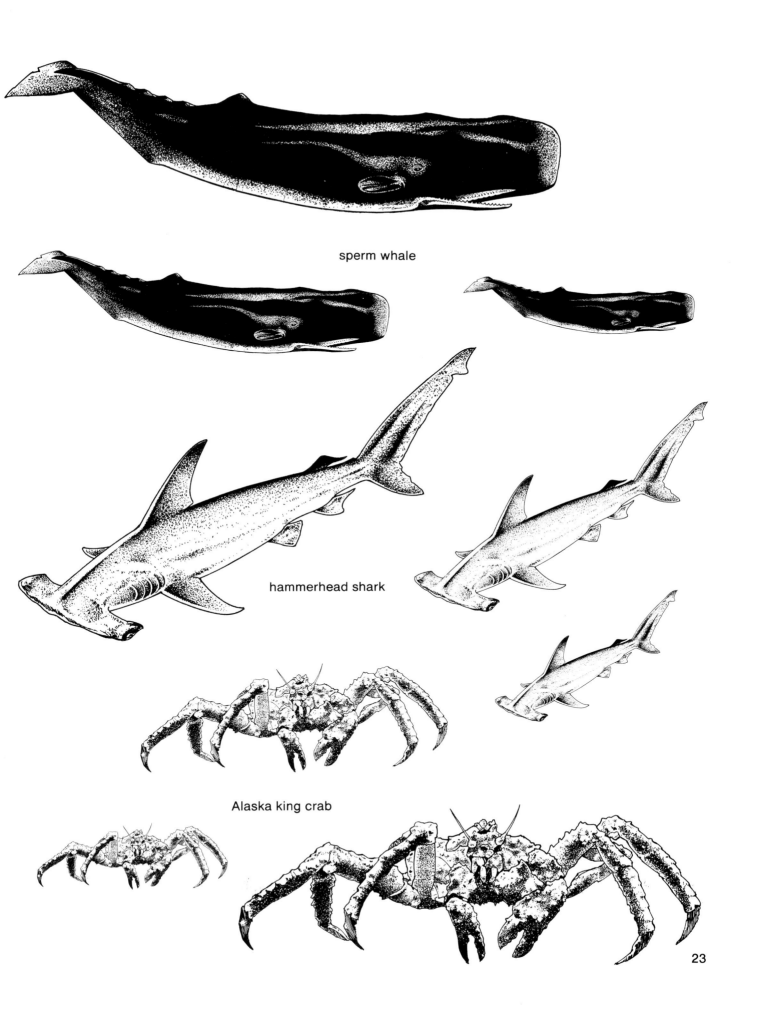

sperm whale

hammerhead shark

Alaska king crab

flying fish

killer whale

whelk

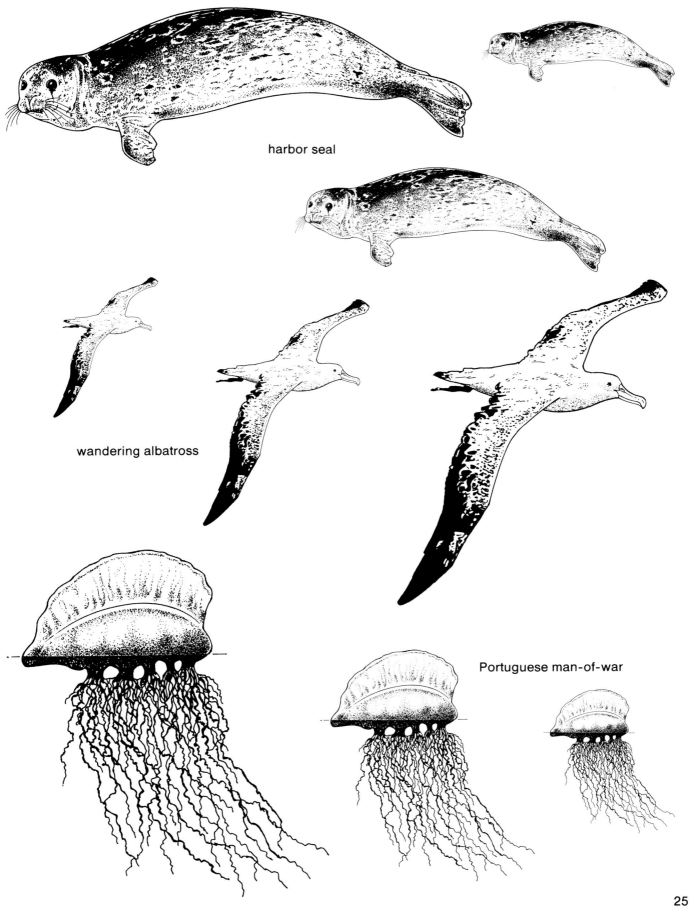

harbor seal

wandering albatross

Portuguese man-of-war

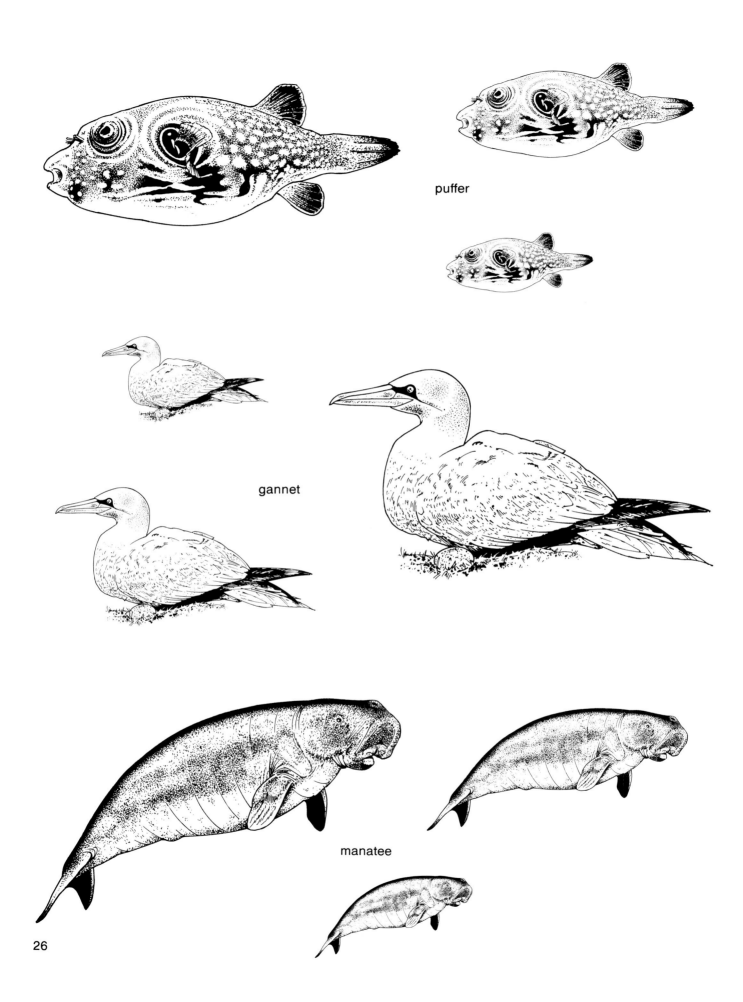

puffer

gannet

manatee

26

manta ray

fur seal

pink salmon

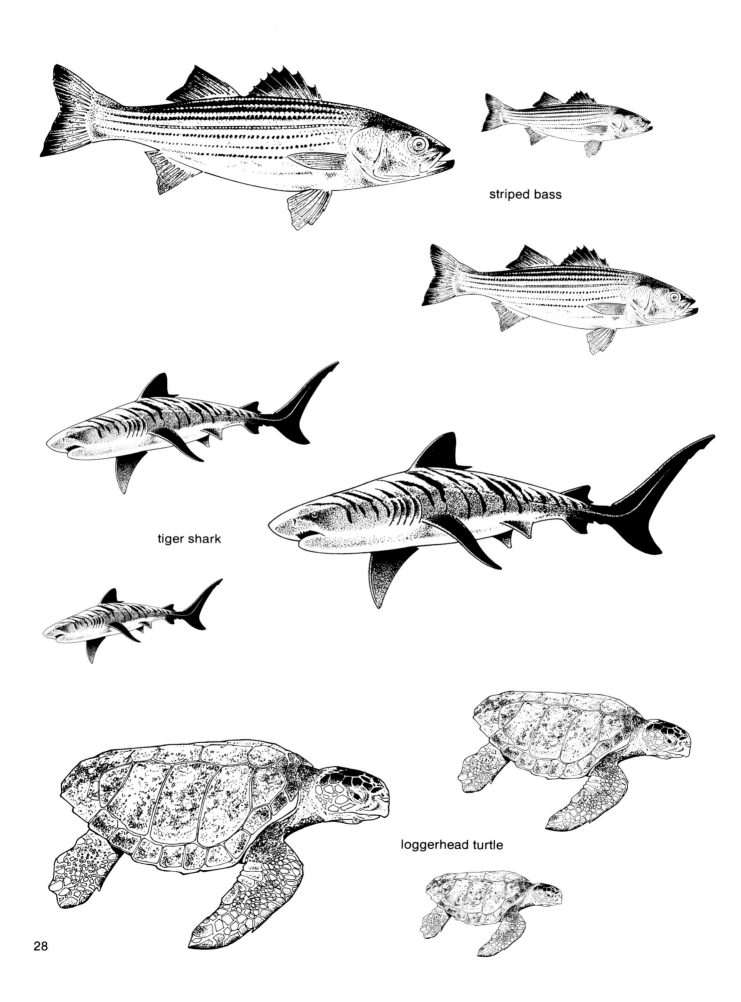

striped bass

tiger shark

loggerhead turtle

gray whale

cormorant

blue marlin

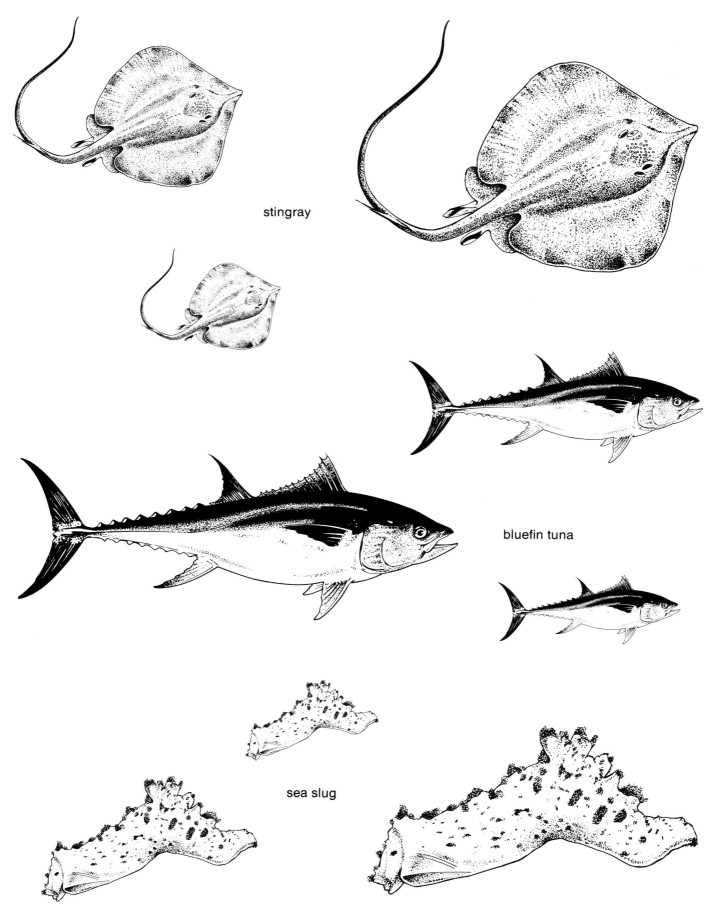

stingray

bluefin tuna

sea slug

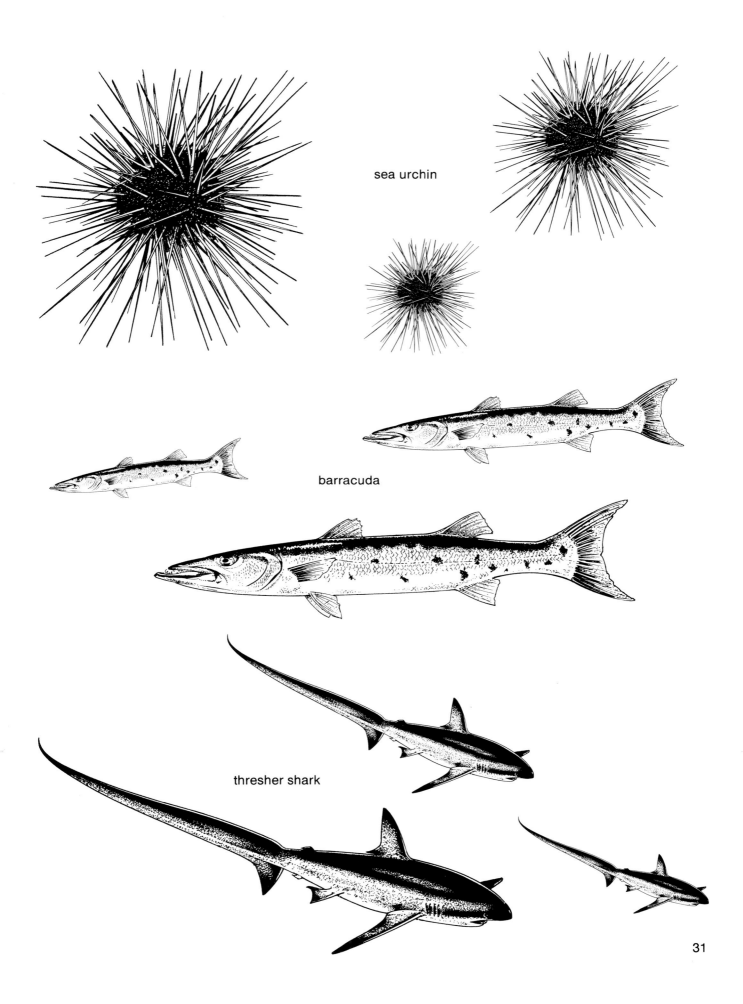

sea urchin

barracuda

thresher shark

31